The Black Woman's Plight: The Constructivism of Identity

The Black Woman's Plight: Constructivism of Identity

The Black Woman's Plight: The Constructivism of
Identity

In dedication to Lameleanique Bates for the

title, The Black Woman's Plight. In our

discussion of my interests in finding the

wholesome conclusions of my dissertation

theme of the Black Woman's Value became the

Black Woman's Plight.

The Black Woman's Plight: The Constructivism of
Identity

I want to thank you Momma for not giving up

on me. I want to thank my Creator for not

giving up on me. I want to thank all my family

members who have loved me. Love ones thank

you. ~K.L.M, MABC, 2014

The Black Woman's Plight: The Constructivism of Identity

The Mathematical Elements (evidence) of

Linguistics Series

The Black Woman's Plight: The Constructivism of
Identity

...she moves and exists...

The Black Woman's Plight: The Constructivism of
Identity

The Journey of the Constructivism Identity

The Black Woman's Plight: The Constructivism of Identity

Discussion Two, Module One: Family vs.

Individual Therapy

Keisha L. Merchant, Discussion with Mark

Hodnick Message on Family and Individual

Therapy Differences

Abstract

This methodology of discourse is built

on the process of personal calculations using

the personal experience from profile, the

discussion case by the author, and the discourse

of the reader, which I have used several

mentors that made similar cases, in the

The Black Woman's Plight: The Constructivism of
Identity

evidence of communications and the journey of

therapy in communications.

Introduction

The reason why I highlight the author's concept

is to show the main theme that I used to connect

all the elements for the author's case. Mark,

your case, and after highlighting the theme that

I received in message and conclusions, I begin

my own process of synthesis and analysis.

Thank you.

These are my highlights in your case:

The Black Woman's Plight: The Constructivism of Identity

Three essential differences that distinguish family therapy and individual therapy from each other include: (a) a systems approach to family therapy, (b) that family therapy is commonly multigenerational, and (c) it focuses on how the nuclear family functions as an emotional unit and how the interrelationships among the family members governs the behavior of each member. (Hodnick, 2014)

Instead, individuals are interconnected as a part of the family system. Within the family system, each member has a role and a set of rules from which predictable patterns of behavior emerge.

The Black Woman's Plight: The Constructivism of Identity

These patterns can either lead to stability, or homeostasis, within the family system or dysfunction. (genpro.com, 2014)

 In a clinical milieu family therapy would be indicated in cases when: "(1) scapegoating systems where the symptom is essential to the family homeostasis; (2) enmeshed families where the communications are confused and diffuse; (3) paranoid-schizoid families where the family denies the symptoms and (4) families in a current acute shared crisis" (Elton, p. 193). As an example, family therapy would be indicated in an enmeshed family where there exist difficulties in communication and where

individuals are not able to speak for themselves

and identify their own feelings. Individual

therapy is indicated when: "the patient has

suffered traumatic separations; (2) separate help

is asked for; (3) the therapist considers

individuation necessary and (4) unusual life

experience" (*ibid,* p.193). An example would

be a case in which one of the members of the

family has been so traumatized or so deprived

that he or she cannot share therapy with the

other members of the family.

The Black Woman's Plight: The Constructivism of
Identity

Methodology and Calculations

Hello Mark. How are you this evening? I

wanted to take the time to read over your

profile. I think it is very important to get to

know a person before commenting on their

post. I hope you do not mind me connecting

your profile with the comments I will make

over the season that I respond to your posts. I

understand that in our lesson for this week, our

module had some very interesting components

about diversity and the level of diversity. I

noticed that you have a rich history in your

The Black Woman's Plight: The Constructivism of Identity

culture and as a family. I understand in our

handbook that people are shaped by their

experiences. The discussion that you presented

on family and individual therapy shows the

dynamics of your background history as an

interactive family member. I noticed that your

focus seem to be driven on solidarity and unity

as a family and individual component into

therapy. This lead me to believe that your

discussion would be based on the networking

system of personal feelings in the relationship

therapies. I understand why your case would

heavily weigh in on personal feelings. The

dynamics of expression can only come through

The Black Woman's Plight: The Constructivism of Identity

a family system that have open expression.

This is an indication to me that your experiences and contributions to the table would involve a family and history of open communication systems. The freedom to express freely and openly, and this is the case you built today. Please correct me if I have misunderstood your case of reason in this week's discussion. Your case seem very well rounded with the stronger case of open communications as an indication into therapy.

Analysis and Discussions

The Black Woman's Plight: The Constructivism of Identity

Over the years, I have found that freedom of expression is not always the case, and in coaching I deal with a range of family and individual dynamics. The family dynamics that I have encountered that have little to any communications are families who externally seem to be the perfect family. It is obvious they do not have any arguments, but the truth of the matter, the test is not the silence, but the individual process of development that is kept hidden and separated from each member. For instance, I coached a young girl who was fighting with eating disorders. It was obvious to me she was wrestling with eating disorders.

The Black Woman's Plight: The Constructivism of Identity

I came to her mother and asked her did she

have any medical conditions. Her mother was

very upset and offended. I worked with this

young girl sixth grader, and she was very quiet.

She was not argumentative. She did

everything I had asked her pertaining to the

sport I was coaching. She moved in weakness.

She could not even hold the ball. The ball was

too heavy. I finally told her, you have to start

eating potatoes to be on my team. Her mother

was offended again. Finally, the first game

arrived. Her whole family came, and I met

everyone. They were quiet, not any

discussions, not any cheering, and I wondered

The Black Woman's Plight: The Constructivism of Identity

at that time why they had lack expression.

Well, I started to coach the daughter through her reality (which I mention in my discussion). I asked the daughter what is life in her life, what food did she eat, what was her portions. The first thing she said, I hate my body. I do not look like the models. Now, I was shock. And, she walked away. By the end of the season, she showed some weight, muscle and strength, she spoke up, and made a basket. The journey was a hard journey. Her mother and family came to games, and started to show expression. The fact is not that I was praised or thanked. But, the process of therapy for her

The Black Woman's Plight: The Constructivism of
Identity

was not a psychotherapy in general I would

suggest, but it was my ability to recognize what

was missing in her life as a member of her

family. I noticed that the reality of the family

network system was not inclusive enough for

her. I think your discussion made me think of

that example. I respect the opportunity to have

"expression" in a communications system, and

the psychotherapy is one of my favorite

therapies. "This learning process will be fully

enhanced if you demonstrate a thirst for

knowledge, a dedication to achieve, and a

willingness to explore differing perspectives.

When you bring these qualities to the academic

The Black Woman's Plight: The Constructivism of Identity

environment of this course, you will be able to not only achieve your immediate professional and personal goals but also build a comprehensive knowledge base that will provide you the tools you need as you progress in your career." (Argosy, 2014, para. 3, Course Review). I thought this course review statement was close to my heart as I read your discussion for this week as a personal reminder that I want to demonstrate a thirst for knowledge and to have the dedication to achieve such diversity in perspective by receiving each person's history and stand point.

The Black Woman's Plight: The Constructivism of
Identity

Conclusions

I thought I would bring up in my discussion the

system of nonverbal communications as an

element to verbal communications in the

dynamics of family and individual therapies for

expressions of internal or external

collections. Carl Jung is one of my favorite

mentors of discourse and Martin Luther King

Jr. I will speak on their influence throughout my

journey as many others. But, what I want to

highlight with Carl Jung and Martin Luther

King Jr. that connect to this discussion is the

ideology around expression and the free

The Black Woman's Plight: The Constructivism of Identity

routines of expression in therapy. Carl Jung building his case of expression for therapy made me realize our unconsciousness struggle in its journey to the forefront of family and individual discourse. Carl Jung spoke on his theories of archetypes. (Stevens, 2006) The second is Martin Luther King Jr. seem to show the struggle of building families when under pressure and crisis as you have stated in your discussion can cause stagnation and regression. Martin Luther King Jr. spoke on this in his sermons and the book, "Why We Can't Wait." (King, 1964) Thank you for the opportunity to read your post.

The Black Woman's Plight: The Constructivism of
Identity

Hodnick, 2014 References

Elton, Anne (1979). Indications for selecting

family or individual therapy. Journal of Family

Therapy, Vol. 1(2), pp.   193-201. Retrieved

from:

http://onlinelibrary.wiley.com/store/10.1046/j..1

979.00493.x/asset/j..1979 .00493.x.pdf?

v=1&t=hs517tw6&s=2329a1276deb1ba0cf5e1

079b45ccc266a 487e27. February 26, 2014.

Family therapy. (n.d.). The American

Heritage® Stedman's Medical Dictionary.

Retrieved from: Dictionary.com

website: http://dictionary.reference.com/browse

/family therapy, February 26, 2014

GenPro (2014). Family Systems

Theory. Retrieved from:

 www.genpro.com/genogram/family- systems-

theory/, February 26, 2014.

The Bowen Center (n.d). Bowen Theory.

Retrieved from:

www.thebowencenter.org/pages/conceptnf.html.

, February/26/2014.

The Black Woman's Plight: The Constructivism of
Identity

Resources

Argosy University, (2014). Marriage & Family

Therapy, Course Review. Retrieved by,

    http://myeclassonline.com

Stevens, Anthony in "The archetypes" (Chapter

3.) Ed. Papadopoulos, Renos. The Handbook of

Jungian   Psychology (2006)

"Why We Can't Wait", *Encyclopedia* (Martin

Luther King, Jr., Research and Education

Institute), accessed 14   November 2012.

Retrieved by, 2014.